Carlson Architects

Expanding Northwestern Regionalism
John Pastier & Donald Carlson

First published in the United States of America by Edizioni Press, Inc.
469 West 21st Street New York, New York 10011, www.edizionipress.com

ISBN: 1-931536-12-0
Library of Congress Catalogue Card Number: 2002101187

Printed in Italy

Design: William van Roden
Design Assistant: Alec Walker
Editor: Aaron Seward
Editorial Assistants: Sarah Palmer, Jamie Schwartz

Carlson Architects

Expanding Northwestern Regionalism
John Pastier & Donald Carlson

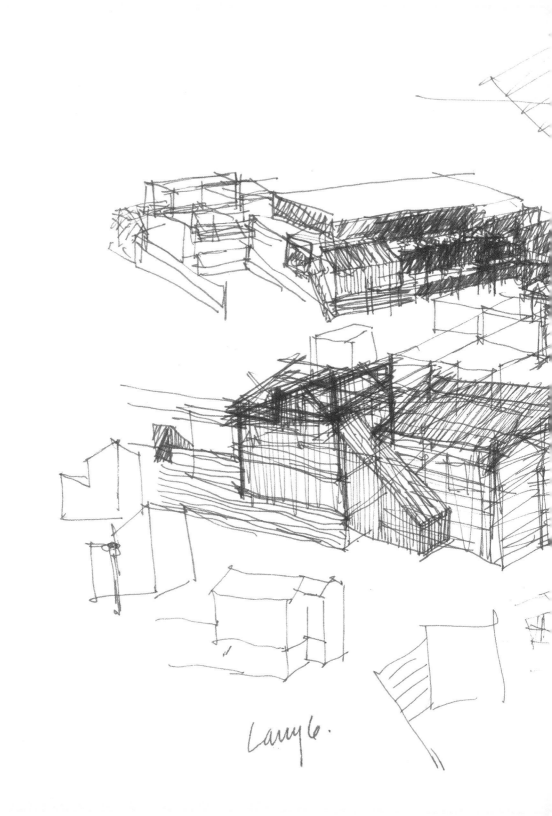

Larry 6.

Larry's Markets

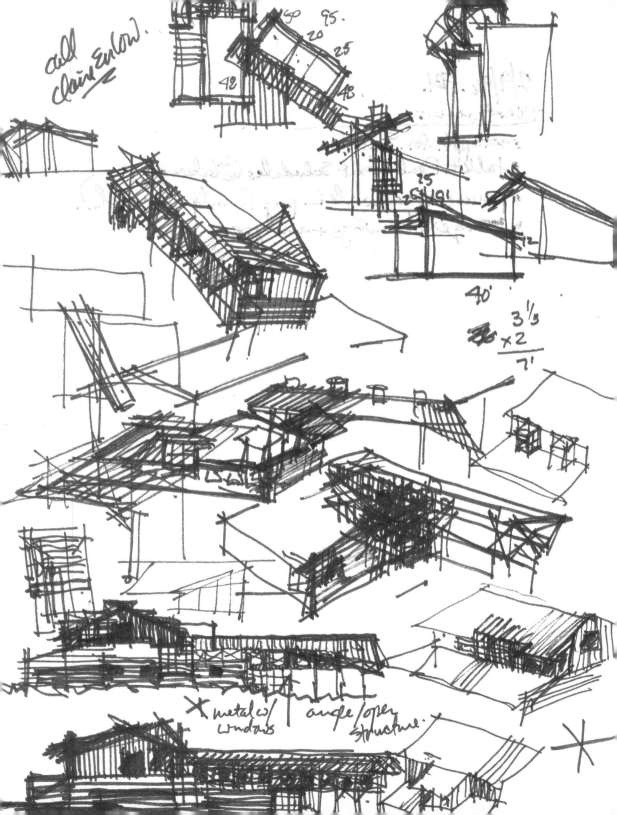

call
Claire Enlow.

150 95.
20
25
48
48

25
25|101
12

40'

$\frac{3\frac{1}{3}}{\times 2}$
$\overline{7'}$

X metal w/
windows

angle/open
structure.

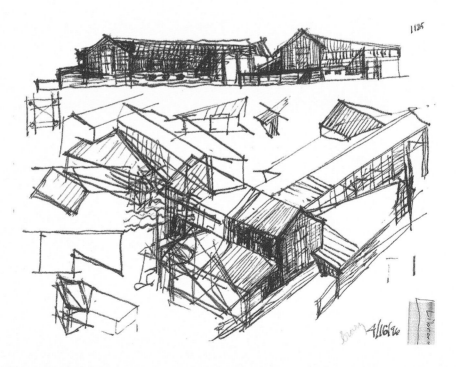

1125

Timberland North Mason Public Library

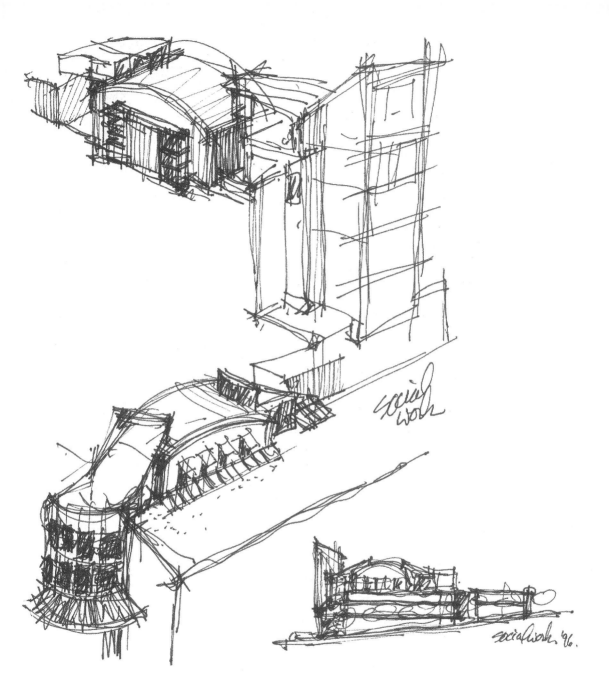

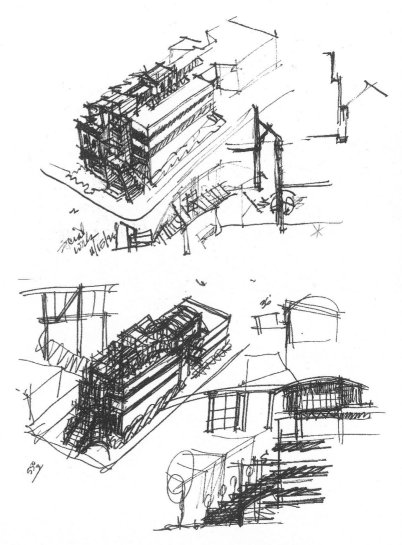

University of Washington School of Social Work Addition

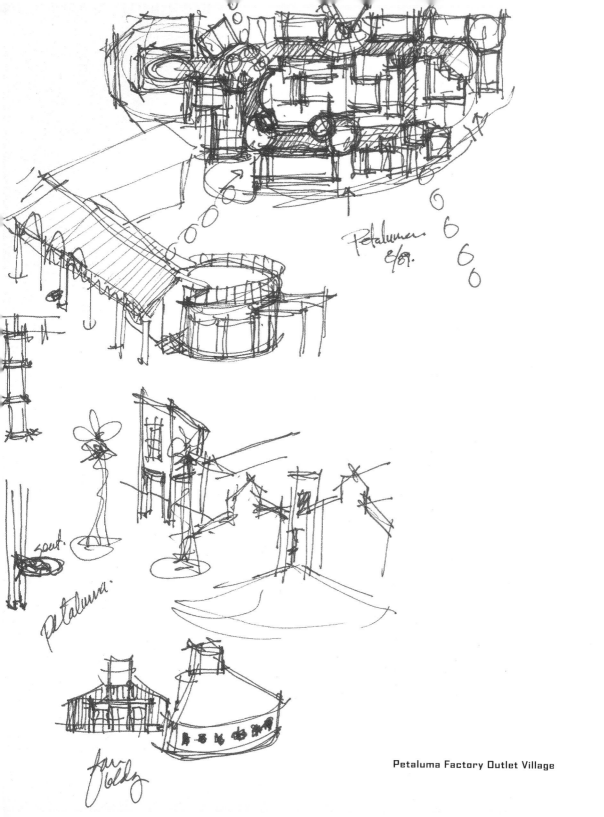

Petaluma Factory Outlet Village

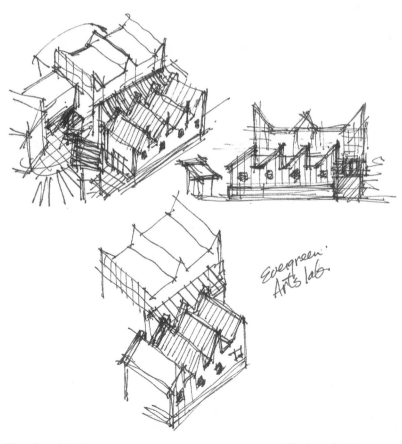

Evergreen
Arts lab.

Evergreen State College Arts Lab Annex

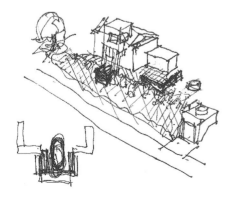

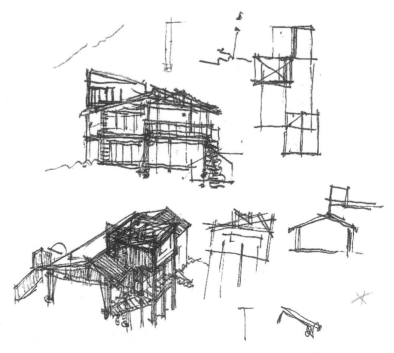

Our architecture is shaped by a desire to create buildings that express the diversity in our world and culture—buildings that vary architecturally because of the inherent differences in places, people, and organizations.

I am continually amazed by the creative diversity in both the man-made and the natural worlds—the unlimited ways to accomplish the same thing—the design of a stairway, for instance. I also admire people who explore the universe of options, people whose work is unpredictable and diverse, people who continue to experiment and evolve. The films of Stanley Kubrick, the buildings of Eero Saarinen, and the architecture of Frank Gehry come to mind.

Variety and spontaneity fuel our design work. We see the design process as an adventure or a journey on which we embark with the intent to create something appropriate and unique—something that will satisfy the client's needs in ways that are unexpected, delightful, and different than we have done before.

We approach each new project with the curiosity of entering the unknown—with a child-like sense of exploration and discovery—a search for delight in each new opportunity and for the traits that will form the personality of the project. We let each design emerge, evolve, and mature. Intuition and spontaneity play a large part in this evolution.

A design can take off in different directions, depending upon the type of project, the context, and the opportunities. We let the project specifics shape and mold the design solution. We look for ways to bring the unexpected to the expected—for subtleties in the definition of a project that will inform our design. No matter how constricting a budget or program or site seems, there is always an opportunity to bring something special to the design that will make the building unique.

This intuitive and open approach to design results in projects that vary in architectural character, and allows us to develop unique solutions for many project types (commercial, institutional, residential, urban design). Today, it is difficult to convince clients that you are, in fact, a generalist architecture firm that designs buildings for people and places, and does not specialize in a building type. Our projects are so diverse people are surprised to find that the same architect was responsible for the design of two projects that are 180 degrees apart in architectural character. There are, however, common underlying themes and threads that link our projects

Design Approach

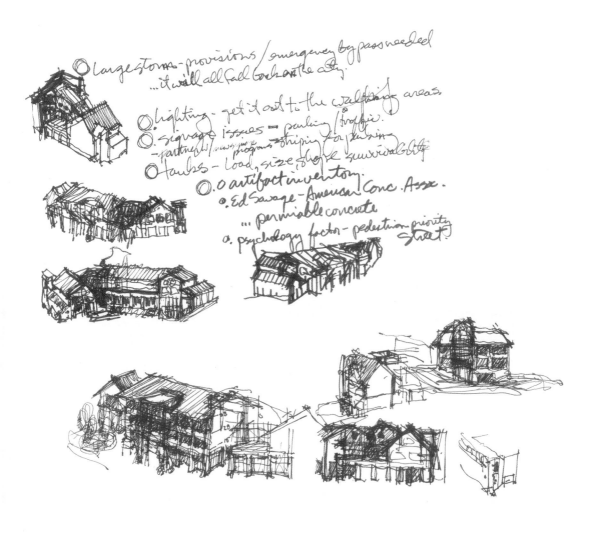

by Donald Carlson

together—whether an addition to an existing campus or a new building that creates its own context.

First, the design of each project is based upon a strong concept, which is integral to the place and the program. Second, there are compositional similarities—the way buildings are organized two-dimensionally in plan and assembled three-dimensionally in form. We use simple materials, usually natural ones, in a straightforward manner that expresses the beauty and utility of each material. Details enhance and complete the initial concept—often adding a touch of whimsy or quirkiness. Each project also contains experimental elements, which explore ideas, forms, materials, and details. And light is a major component of our design palette—how natural light plays with forms and enters the building, and how lighting dramatically enhances the architecture.

The basic concept for each project grows from the circumstances that frame the project-client desires, location, budget, feelings, etc. You have to understand the parameters, the obstacles, the opportunities, and the spirit. As you work with a project, you begin to develop a feeling for what the project can be, for its personality. I tell our clients that we are like actors getting into character. First, you need to understand the play and then get into the personality of the role until appropriate responses become automatic and in character. The same is true in the design of a building: you develop a feeling for the appropriate response to each design decision, down to the smallest detail.

In the Larry's Markets,[1] the client said he wanted a "food factory"—a building that would look different than the typical grocery store. The food factory image brought to mind simple, matter-of-fact buildings with exposed structures constructed of basic materials, like concrete blocks and corrugated metal. Therefore, the composition and assembly achieved an aesthetic that was seemingly inevitable, yet eccentric. The markets actually fit perfectly into their messy and gritty suburban strip locations. The design of each new Larry's became easier and more fun. We knew the role, we were in character, and this allowed us to nimbly improvise and develop variations on the theme, to accommodate the owner's evolving ideas, and to fit each site and context. The industrial aesthetic developed in the markets is limitless in its design variations, massing, and materials palette; there are no rules.

[1]   [2]   [3]

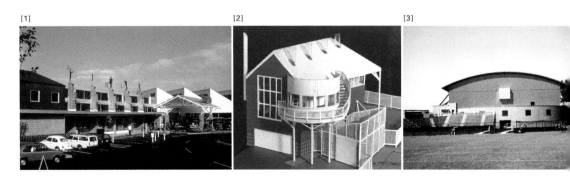

The markets led to many interesting and diverse projects for clients attracted to the industrial aesthetic. An "industrial loft house" [2] for an art collector was clad in black asphalt shingles and corrugated galvanized metal. An oil tank-like room, wrapped by a stairway to the roof deck, notches into a corner of the main house block and smokestack-shaped skylights line the roof. We also applied the aesthetic for a compound of waterfront lodging units and boat storage. The units were stacked in metal-clad towers separated by black asphalt shingle "shadow" elements. And, at the University of Washington, the lessons learned from Larry's about scaling down the appearance of a large "box" were used in the design of a sports practice facility that housed an indoor football field and track.[3]

Our experimentation with the industrial aesthetic continues to evolve. Recent projects have become more lyrical in their forms, using shapes that are more organic and combinations of elements that both blend and contrast with their surroundings. The University Child Development School addition, the University of Washington School of Social Work addition, [4] the Bellwether project, [5] and the Ballard Lofts illustrate the design evolution.

Designing projects for campuses with an existing architectural style is a challenge. Our approach is to preserve and enhance the existing campus by designing new structures that are sympathetic to the existing architecture and help shape outdoor spaces. Getting into character, we analyze the existing architecture to understand the scale, materials, and forms. We are then able to develop design variations on the campus theme that express particular functions and develop the personality of the new building. At Lakeside School in Seattle, a Georgian Colonial campus, we designed an addition to the historic refectory. The addition blends into the campus with similar shapes, materials, and details, but also has unique design features that expand the campus vernacular and create a distinctive "personality" for the building.

Sometimes we get the opportunity to invent an off-the-wall project—like the Santa Claus house for the central plaza in downtown Seattle. The conceptual idea was to create a "Lilliputian" Christmas scene around the mayor's Christmas tree. We designed a cluster of large-scale "toys" with a full size sailboat and a truck packed with colorful presents. Santa was housed in a large clear snow globe element and the photographer was located in a jack-in-the-box. [6]

[4]

[5]

[6]

For us, development of the design concept is a fluid process that explores alternatives for organizing, orienting, and creating individual elements in plan, and for connecting and assembling the elements into a three-dimensional composition.

Plan organization is based on program relationships but is also influenced by adjacent geometries, views, and natural orientation. Our work with clusters of multiple buildings and objects in urban areas and campuses has greatly influenced how we organize both the interiors and exteriors of individual buildings.

The Bellwether project began as a master plan exercise, which resulted in a cluster of waterfront buildings around a public square and park at the end of the peninsula. The buildings are configured in plan to shape and frame the outdoor spaces. The "bending" geometry creates buildings with multiple views and fronts.

Timberland library [7] is a good example of a dynamic interior space created by shifting axes that orient to both street and forest. The building is composed as a cluster of connected individual elements, like a compound.

Plans are an inclusive composition of all adjacent elements. For the public areas at a sports park, we designed the small buildings that housed the facilities and the related fencing enclosures. The plan includes the building (rest rooms and snack bar), the chain link fencing that encircles the tot lot and screens the volleyball court, and a line of trees that shade the outdoor eating area. Seemingly unrelated elements are tightly clustered together to create interconnected spaces and give the small building a greater physical presence.

Three-dimensionally, our buildings are put together as an assembly of parts—sometimes loosely connected as in a compound, and other times tightly connected as in joinery. Building elements tend to be simple shapes, and some of the most interesting assemblies combine dissimilar elements. Elements are combined in a variety of ways, such as colliding and interlocking, to form complex three-dimensional assemblies. Combining dissimilar elements also animates the building roofline to form a skyline.

Larry's and the School of Social Work are good illustrations of the variety of massing and scale made possible by interconnected building elements. The entry façade of Larry's Market in Bellevue, for instance, combines a tall octagonal silver element that links

[7] [8]

with a shiny green box element and flying canopy, which angles off of a long, tall, oblong element.[8] At the University of Washington Social Work building, a cluster of interlocking, metal-clad elements appears to be a rooftop village.[9]

Another good example of joinery in a more traditional building is the fine-arts addition to an existing classroom building at the Lakeside School. A new L-shaped building was strategically positioned opposite to the existing L-shaped building, thus creating a sculpture courtyard at the heart of the expanded facility. The seemless addition complements the existing architecture.

We use natural materials and a wide variety of less expensive industrial materials because they are durable and possess a simple beauty. They are sculptural materials. Natural materials also age gracefully, developing a patina and requiring little maintenance. Concrete block has a scale, rhythm, and natural concrete texture. Natural galvanized metal has a spectral light quality that glows even in the dimmest light—which is especially beneficial in the Pacific Northwest. And when corrugated or shaped, galvanized metal has a corduroy dark/light shadow pattern. [10]

How a material is used is very important—we clad individual elements in different materials to achieve the desired effects of contrast and collage—for instance, solid and grounded versus light and floating. Combining contrasting materials allow us to manipulate the proportions of walls and building elements. Many of the "use of materials" lessons and techniques evident in our work today were developed during the design of the Larry's Markets.[11]

We experiment with material installation details also. For the Timberland Library, we wanted the main reading room block to glow in the forest so we clad it with corrugated galvanized metal. To further diminish the scale of the material, we lapped the sheets in four-foot bands, as in beveled siding. An elderly citizen of the community said that the building reminded her of the old outhouses, which were clad in long "royal" shingles—creating the same scale effect. We had unknowingly tapped into the real context and history of the community.

The proper use of the right materials and appropriate details to support and enhance the concept are essential in a successful design. We like to include details that not only fit the basic concept and character but also add a sense of eccentricity, uniqueness,

[9]   [10]   [11]

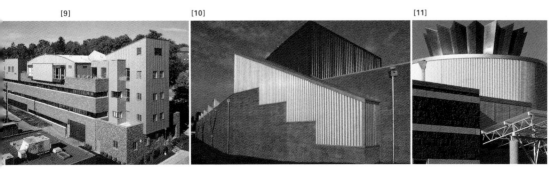

and playfulness. At the Lakeside Arts Building [12] a handrail is sculpture, at University Preparatory Academy a column twists mysteriously, and at the Shilshole Marina office building canopies zigzag to the entry. [13]

In architecture there is the use of natural light and there is lighting—both can make or break the design of a building. Natural light brings shape and glow to architecture and life to interior spaces. Our projects use natural light to the fullest. Light is brought in through gaps, cracks, and sawtooth roofs. The markets are ringed with clerestory windows that bring daylight into the middle of each store. Timberland library has a central skylight that allows light to filter down through roof framing members into the heart of the library. At the Evergreen College sculpture facility, no artificial lighting is needed during the day to use the shop or to fabricate sculpture. [14]

We incorporate indirect lighting or a component of up-lighting into the ambient lighting scheme of all our projects. Indirect lighting is comfortable for the human eye, accentuating the volume of internal spaces and producing a lantern-like glow at night. Larry's Markets are entirely up-lit with industrial metal halide fixtures, which also benefits their 24-hour business.

Many of our projects incorporate the "glowing lantern" idea to create a safe harbor or warm hearth effect. The ultimate glowing lantern is the Kobe temporary community center project, which is a translucent corrugated fiberglass clad structural frame—a welcoming sign for the Kobe citizens after the earthquake.

Lighting, for us, is also experimental. The effect of the light, the drama it creates is the most important aspect in lighting design, not the fixture. Lighting is integrated with the building design. Our goal is to make the fixtures as invisible or as unobtrusive as possible. The Carlson and Wilcher loft houses offer good examples of experimental lighting techniques. We wanted to achieve the most dramatic lighting effects using the least expensive fixtures, and to experiment with the effects of lighting in combination with industrial materials. The dramatic lighting effects that can be achieved with hidden spotlights in inexpensive mounts or bare bulbs behind punched metal panels belie their humble sources. [15]

Good architecture will work on every level—from the initial conceptual ideas to the last detail. The design journey is intense, long, winding, and filled with

[12]   [13]

surprises. There is a definite sequence and pace. And you know instantly when you've made a design breakthrough—Aha!!!

Our design sequence begins with the act of getting into character—understanding the forces that will drive the project, shaping the design, and getting a feel for the essence of the building. Understanding the essence, the opportunities, and the constraints leads to development of the basic concept that will guide every design decision along the way.

Once the concept is established, the actual building design takes shape—first in plan and massing. We work from the inside-out and the outside-in, playing with plan geometries and element forms that will satisfy the program, relate to the context, and enhance the concept. A feeling for appropriate materials and patterns begins to become evident as the building forms emerge. We look for opportunities to experiment with materials and shapes to create the eccentricities, the unique elements and details that will form the personality of the building. The use of light is an integral ingredient in our architecture—how shapes work in light, how shapes let light into the building, and how lighting enhances interior forms.

Designing is like popping popcorn—it takes awhile to get a feel for the character of the project until the kernel of the first breakthrough idea pops and then the ideas come fast and furious!

There is a chronological sequence of projects that forms the backbone and identity of our firm's work, starting with the industrial aesthetic of the early Larry's Markets and extending to current projects that contain more lyrical aesthetics and combinations of materials. The feature projects in this monograph follow that chronological sequence. ■

[14]   [15]

One of the most evocative images of American urbanism is a 19th century photograph of a street in upper Manhattan. It shows a dozen row houses of modest grandeur, all four stories tall and three windows wide, built of brick and trimmed with stone. Each is capped by a bold cornice, and has an imposing flight of balustraded stone stairs leading to its grandly framed front door.

What makes this image memorable is that the row houses don't form a continuous streetscape, but sit as isolated clumps in space—three together, then a gap wide enough for six or eight more, then another three. Visible through the gap, a block or two in the distance, is a tier of six others. Unlike any other New York street scene, this view is dominated by empty space, unbuilt and devoid of vegetation and people. The streets are not even paved; the real city is yet to come. In a sense, the emptiness and silence of this vista prefigures some of the paintings of Edward Hopper and Giorgio di Chirico.

Although this photo portrays an unoccupied and incomplete quarter, it strongly suggests optimism. Small entrepreneurs came upon a blank urban canvas, envisioned a finished neighborhood and took the first steps to create one. They developed as much property as their resources allowed, confident that others would follow their cues and complete the pattern.

Today, five generations later and on the opposite end of the country, a modest pedestrian mews traverses an outdoor shopping center in a prosperous Seattle suburb. It connects a row of small shop-fronts to a sidewalk flanking a busy vehicular street. When this landscaped passage was built, its designer knew that it would not serve any major immediate purpose; pedestrians are rare in suburbia. But he planned it optimistically—even more so than the Manhattan townhouse builders—hoping that its example might eventually inspire others to continue the pattern and create a more humanly scaled, pedestrian oriented suburban townscape.

This small but symbolic gesture is the work of Donald Carlson. A native of Kansas City, Carlson studied architecture and began his professional apprenticeship in the Midwest. In 1970 he moved to the Pacific Coast, where he earned his graduate degree at UCLA, drawn there by their urban design based program. While in school and afterwards he worked for Frank Gehry, and other Los Angeles and San Francisco architects before opening his own practice in Seattle in 1983. He brings many strengths to the design process, but two are especially conspicuous. One is an inherent optimism. Carlson is an artist who often works with building types and budgetary niches where

An Architecture of Optimism

Silas A. Holmes, ca. 1877; negative number 36173;
Collection of The New-York Historical Society

and Flexibility by John Pastier

artistry is rarely possible. Unfazed, he operates under the conviction that there is expressive potential in modest, mundane, and even messy assignments, and he is able to uncover well-hidden possibilities for expression, completion, and connectivity—whether those possibilities are between old and new elements of additive projects, or between a new building and an existing context.

His other major strength is an unusual design flexibility, and this makes it difficult to characterize his architecture simply or with complete consistency. He could be seen with considerable justification as a non-dogmatic modernist, but he has sometimes undertaken commissions [1] that called for traditionalist exterior expression, and has respected that call with an open-mindedness that hard-line modernists would never be able to muster. In many ways he is a conscious regionalist, but his regionalism is interpretive rather than literal, situation-specific rather than formulaic, and in some respects it is one that redirects and redefines the local sensibility rather than following it unquestioningly. [2] He is sensitive to his milieu, yet his playfulness and sense of visual adventure are not qualities that are the norm in the architecturally conservative region where he practices.

Carlson says that he is "good at osmosis and taking in influences," and speaks of "getting into the role" when he designs. This can be challenging for clients to visualize if they are seeking a predictable signature style and a foreordained architectural response. In getting into his roles, he is more like Dustin Hoffman than Woody Allen, and more like Alec Guiness than John Wayne. He doesn't portray himself as much as he aspires to bring out the essence of his part, and play off the other members of the cast.

Keeping this versatility in mind, we may now consider Donald Carlson's essential tendencies and personal values as a designer—the qualities that give form and direction to his optimism and flexibility.

Immediate Context

Contextual sensitivity is an inherent Carlson trait, and at its best it embraces both the physical and cultural aspects of the building site and its community. With nearly all of his commissions located in northern California and the Pacific Northwest, he has long ago learned to deal with difficult sloping sites, auto-oriented environments, local vegetation, and occasionally even native forest. [3] He refers to topography as "the third dimension in planning," and

[1]   [2]

has used it deftly in buildings for Evergreen State University and the Lakeside School to gain maximum interior space without excessive visual bulk. His project for the University Child Development School will employ a similar strategy. At the Port of Bellingham, Carlson went a step further by creating a topographic context on a flat artificial peninsula, where he built underground parking and manipulated the grades around it, thereby creating a raised public plaza with enhanced water views as well as topological relief.

Many of his commissions involve adding to existing structures or groups of buildings: sometimes grafting on to them, sometimes knitting them together, sometimes transforming them, and sometimes emulating their spirit if not their literal form. Often, the result is a remarkable synthesis in which the previous design is greatly improved by the new one, as Carlson is able to intuit a latent expressive or experiential potential not fully realized in the original. Indeed, this ability to sense opportunities for completion and closure is at the heart of much of his work. [4]

At times he has been asked to design a building type inherently at odds with its setting, such as the Oak Tree Larry's Market, a 45,000-square-foot "big box" whose rear faced a small-scaled residential street. There, he was careful to locate truck loading on a less sensitive side of the building, and detail and landscape the inevitable blank wall in a dignified way that respected the existing nature of the streetscape. In the case of an even larger big box, the Totem Lake Larry's Market in an eastern Seattle suburb, the architect prides himself on having created "a four-sided-building"—one that responds to different environmental conditions with four differently composed faces, including a lively, well-articulated, but essentially solid rear wall facing a busy freeway.

In schools such as Overlake, Lakeside, and University Prep, existing campus patterns and architectural styles dictated careful visual adaptation, or even the adoption of a style outside Carlson's normal range of modern expression. In those cases, the exteriors are deferential and accommodating, with inventive visual gestures primarily located inside, where their presence is doubly welcome because they are somewhat unexpected. [5]

Broader Context

These are all examples of response to immediate physical context, an important tool in any designer's repertoire to be sure, but also one that can reliably be found in the upper strata of the profession. Sensitivity and response to the wider physical and cul-

[3]   [4]   [5]

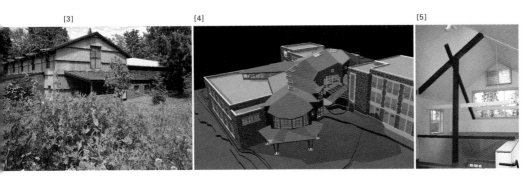

tural context—the genius loci, if you will—is less common and arguably more important. Early in his design process, Carlson often assembles "character boards"—photo-essays of not only immediate context, but also of interesting local buildings, materials, details, and natural features—to be used as visual and intellectual resources in the design process.

In the Petaluma Factory Outlet Village, this process allowed him to develop a visual vocabulary based on the local commercial and agricultural vernacular, sometimes reflecting specific buildings and sometimes abstracted common elements of such structures. The exterior cladding of the Timberland library is a grandly over-scaled metal version of the wood shingles that were logged and manufactured in the region for generations; in addition, abstracted tree motifs are part of the interior walls and external structure. At Bellwether, steel bents supporting canopies on the central plaza derive their shape from shipping cranes in the harbor.[6] And in the wonderfully light, unbuilt competition-winning design for community pavilions in Kobe, the architect was clearly inspired by the refined wood building traditions of Japan.

Carlson's strong urbanistic impulse also falls under this heading. In his master planning and urban design commissions, he creates a large-scale order that in itself becomes context. This can be seen in the village-like arrangement of buildings at Petaluma, as well as the shaping of its perimeter parking zone. In the Bellwether master plan, he creates an asymmetric, vista-driven urban order, complete with major civic open space, on virgin soil. At a smaller scale, in the Growing Vine Street project, he collaborates with environmental artist Buster Simpson to create a multi-block water feature and greenway in a dense emerging downtown residential neighborhood. And the Larry's Market complex in Bellevue is the site of the previously mentioned mews that may someday become the nucleus of a larger pedestrian circulation system.

Light

In the Northwest, natural light is a variable and precious commodity. Winter days are brief and largely overcast or rainy, while summer's long 16-hour days are often, but not reliably, filled with the bright, sharp sunlight that is taken for granted in California and the Mediterranean. Carlson invariably finds ways to introduce daylight in its varied forms to his interiors, not only horizontally through oversized windows and internal borrowed lights, but from above through skylights, clerestories, sawtooth roofs, "light scoops," and translucent roof panels. When

[6] [7]   [8]

possible, he deploys artificial light indirectly to produce soft illumination that resembles north daylight, and he will often blend natural light with electrical illumination. He likes to use industrial fixtures both for their high output and for their inherent character as objects. In his Bellwether office building, he introduced small pools of daylight to an underground parking garage through glass block prisms that were part of the plaza paving above.

Structure

Virtually all of the architect's projects are located in the Pacific coast seismic zone, which demands more robust structural systems than those found elsewhere in the country. Carlson likes to reveal these structures wherever possible, and, beyond that, takes delight in detailing and displaying their joints and connections. Exposed trusses, whether of steel or heavy timber, give scale and form to several of his large interior spaces. [7] Exterior and interior steel framing is often angled, bent, or drilled for expressive purposes, or put prominently on display. In remodeling both the Wilcher and Carlson houses, portions of the floors and interior walls were selectively removed to reveal the underlying wood framing pattern, open up internal spaces, connect them visually, and create a rich layering of permeable surfaces. [8]

Materials

Carlson's project budgets usually dictate economy of cladding and finish, and thus his preferred palette of materials is inexpensive, though possessive of strong inherent character. He calls these "natural" and "manufactured natural." The latter includes corrugated galvanized metal, factory-painted metal, metal shingles, asphalt shingles, split-faced and smooth concrete block, exposed wood trusses, exposed steel structure, lightly stained plywood, perforated metal ceilings that can transmit light and air, and rolling fiberglass doors that can transmit light. [9] These are chosen for their visual and tactile richness, their texture, inherent color, and reflectivity.

Form

Carlson's buildings take on a wide variety of forms, as would be expected given the flexibility of his design approach. Two of his largest projects, the Ballard Lofts and the Indoor Sports Practice Facility for the University of Washington, are simple and understated in shape, while some of the mid-sized and smaller ones, including the Wilcher and Carlson houses, the Bellwether office buildings, and the University Child Development School, are three-dimensional-

[9]

ly complex, playful, and in places surprising. Some of these designs are exuberant and even startling, such as the Timberland Library, the Sonics Practice Facility, the additions to the UW School of Social Work, and the bright, warped-surface awnings of the Shilshole Bay Marina remodeling. Consciously or unconsciously, Carlson seems to have an impulse to provide liveliness in most of the small and mid-size works, while cloaking the largest ones in calmness and modesty, allowing the buildings' magnitude, simple volumes, and inherent proportions to make the primary expressive statements.

Color

While many regional architects (including many of the very best) respond to northwestern light by exploring the subtleties of myriad monochromatic shades and tones, Carlson's approach to color is usually more full-blooded. A good case can be made for rich colors as combatants of the psychological effects of a gray climate. Beyond that, some of his color schemes carry symbolic or contextual meaning. His Seattle Supersonics Practice Facility uses the basketball team's colors of green and red, combined with silvery metal, to make an appropriately bold statement alongside a busy urban highway. His extremely economical remodeling of the Shilshole Marina created playfully shaped fabric awnings whose yellow color matched various bright safety-painted elements found on the premises. In his own house, he used black as a velvety backdrop color, sparingly inside and abundantly outside. In the University Prep expansion, key circulation nodes are assigned unique rich colors to provide orientation clues within a complex pattern of corridors. Carlson's color palette is sometimes more muted, most notably in the Timberland library, where the tones are restrained in order not to compete with the unusual vigor and complexity of the building's forms, spaces, and displayed structure.

Regionalsim

On the whole, these tendencies combine to create a form of regional architecture, but it is a complex and personal regionalism that transcends the usual local definition of the word. Emerging in the decades after World War II, Pacific Northwest regionalism was, until recently, a softened, laid-back form of modernism; a design approach that emphasized woodsy "natural" materials, sometimes flirted with rusticity, and dictated restraint in form and color. Gray and beige tones predominated in response to a climate where rain is frequent and sunlight is usually muted. (There is a local saying that any color is acceptable here as long as it's one that can be found on the underside of a mushroom.) The Northwest is a place of near-legendary politeness and civility, traits that have permeated local architecture and were also aligned with cultural conservatism and conformism, and even a degree of provincialism. In architecture, recapitulation and refinement were embraced more naturally than innovation and playfulness.

For all its care in fitting into its context, Carlson's architecture, in its adventurousness and invention, is also at odds with a strong local tendency toward architectural reticence. His use of industrial materials and visual devices of strong color and angular, dynamic forms mark him as a bit of an iconoclast. "I don't consider myself a radical, but all of our projects push the envelope somewhere, even subtly," he observes. (Interestingly, on a personal level, Carlson is virtually indistinguishable from the quintessential long-established Seattleite: invariably self-effacing, soft-spoken, understated, neatly groomed, and favoring well-pressed white shirts, even when wearing blue jeans.)

But his perceived position as a nonconformist is gradually changing as his sensibilities enter the local mainstream, both through the output of other design architects consciously or unconsciously influenced by his work, and also through its dissemination on a more vernacular level. The local use of metal has become more common, perhaps because it is now more generally perceived as "cool," and as an appropriate material for a region that is home to so many high-tech enterprises. (Of course, this connection could have easily been made long ago, since Seattle has been a hub of the aircraft industry for about eight decades.) So too has the use of overt color become less unusual in local buildings. In these senses, Carlson has contributed to a broadening of the boundaries of northwestern regionalism, abetted by other changes in Seattle's social and cultural landscape.

It was inevitable that a city so enamored of strong coffee would become more open to intense stimuli of other types. Carlson's colors and materials might be seen as the architectural equivalent of Seattle's more evolved forms of caffeine—varied and carefully prepared. While the city is still showing its conservatism in many of its new civic and cultural buildings, it is also the locus of some heady architectural experiments that tend to position Carlson in the middle of the road—where, of course, he always has been if judged by architectural standards more worldly than Seattle's. He has been quickly rendered a centrist by locally built works of Steven Holl and Frank Gehry, and a distinctly radical Rem Koolhaas central library now under construction. Holl has executed a suburban art museum whose concrete walls are painted red, and whose exterior metal panels act as screens for multimedia projections. Gehry, Carlson's old mentor, has produced an all-metal rock-and-roll museum whose intense unconventional colors and vigorously undulating forms make Carlson's boldest designs seem absolutely subdued.

Thanks to these designers from Los Angeles, New York, and Rotterdam, Donald Carlson has been revealed as a centrist architect of and for the new Seattle, a city that is slowly, and sometimes painfully, shedding its architectural inhibitions.■

Larry's Markets Seattle

Washington Metropolitan Area

In 1984, Larry and Suzi McKinney asked Carlson Architects to design a new grocery store that would look different than any typical grocery store in Seattle. They described their vision for Larry's Market as a "food factory."

The first store was located in a new retail center called Oak Tree Village, north of downtown Seattle. The Oak Tree design established the conceptual ideas, architectural character, and materials palette that would become the hallmarks of Larry's Markets' architectural image. The Oak Tree Larry's created a unique prototype for three subsequent stores.

The architects designed Larry's Markets in Kirkland, Bellevue, and Tukwila as site-specific variations on the theme established at Oak Tree. While the markets varied in size, the program for each store was the same. As Larry said initially, "Don't forget, we are a grocery store." The program required a basic pattern of central rows of shelving surrounded by specialty departments, with checkout stands at the front of the store. This decided, the challenge became how to create a unique image and architecture that would distinguish Larry's from other supermarkets.

Before launching into design for the first store at Oak Tree, Carlson researched grocery stores and traditional marketplaces. From his travels in Europe and regular visits to Seattle's Pike Place Market, he knew that traditional markets are inherently intriguing places. The obvious question was "Why are grocery stores not as enjoyable or as interesting as traditional marketplaces?" Keeping the general program requirements in mind and determining architectural strength and visible activity as the exciting aspects of a marketplace, Carlson analyzed existing Larry's Markets and other local groceries to determine which aspects of the stores could be used.

Concepts developed during the initial investigation and design studies evolved to become the architectural character that make the look and feel of Larry's Markets distinct. The design highlights visual activities. The entry and front sidewalks are enlivened by diverse building shapes that house independent functions, such as cafés, flower shops, and espresso bars. The sequence of individual building elements creates a village-scale image for the front of the market. Inside, the departments are designed as a series of individual elements as well, reflecting the diversity found in traditional marketplaces. Interior designer, Suzi McKinney, created a unique image for each department with custom valences, signage, and details. Seafood departments

Oak Tree Village, 1986

Above: A flower shop enhances the store's prominent entry, which is indirectly lit with industrial metal halide fixtures. Below: A neon apple (the symbol of Larry's Markets) is perched precariously above the corner of the building in a wire mesh covered steel frame, signaling to passing motorists.

have either a school of fish mobile or a real fish tank built into the "O" of seafood. Special lighting, canopies, and large billboard-size murals define the produce departments. Interior lighting is comfortable for shoppers. High bay clerestory windows bring natural light to the heart of the stores, and ambient lighting, provided by indirectly mounted industrial fixtures with metal halide lamps, washes the white painted metal roof decking above with glare-free light. A lantern-like glow emanating from the stores at night is an added benefit of the clerestory windows and indirect lighting system.

Minimizing the height of exterior walls and interior ceilings in the perimeter departments diminishes the "big-box" appearance. The architects lined the raised roofs over central shelving rows with clerestory windows to create an expansive feeling inside. Sculptural architectural elements, visible both day and night, create local landmarks on the skyline. The "food factory" image is enhanced by a palette of simple industrial materials–natural concrete block, glazed block, glass block, exposed structural steel, galvanized corrugated metal siding, and corrugated fiberglass roofing.

The architectural concept for Larry's Market evolved with the design of each new store. The 45,000-square-foot Oak Tree store established the Larry's Markets image with a series of simple gable building forms and a highly visible flower shop at the store's main entry. Industrial materials complement the massing. A large galvanized steel frame cube with neon apples perches precariously on an elevated corner of the building as the dominant feature.

The freestanding Kirkland store, at 65,000 square feet, is located on an interstate freeway interchange, surrounded by suburban strip commercial buildings. The visually prominent site called for a more playful building, with colorful metal building elements (like toy building blocks) inserted into concrete block walls and a large "saw-tooth" café. The design contrasts back to front with an animated fortress facing the freeway and a large transparent façade greeting the customer. The architects created the "skyline" identity with pylons at the front of the store, which are capped by artist Buster Simpson's full-size human wind vanes entitled "The Food Chain."

The Bellevue store, third in the series, is the flagship at 75,000 square feet. The Bellevue project includes two 8,000-square-foot shop buildings in addition to the market. In response to the glass towers of this evolving, sophisticated city, the architecture of the Bellevue store departs from the pitched roof character of the prior two projects. It is sleek, horizon-

Kirkland, 1989
The glowing interior and bold pylons, capped by artist Buster Simpson's
full-size human wind vanes (entitled "The Food Chain"), create a visually
dynamic entry.

tal, and modern. The designers added green glazed block as a new material in the industrial palette. The shop buildings form a gateway at the front of the project and face the market across the central parking area. A collage of eccentric, rounded, flat roof elements of varying heights and a large pleated metal crown create a landmark identity day and night.

While the Bellevue store worked well, the owner realized that it was very expensive to run. He wanted to develop a more cost-effective store of around 55,000 square-feet. In response, Carlson designed Tukwila to be a model in size, food, and services. The design of the Tukwila store reverted back to the Oak Tree store in many ways—especially with the basic architectural forms of simple gable roofs. However, like Kirkland, the store capitalizes on its busy highway location by presenting a dramatic animated façade to the passing motorists.

Larry's Markets established Carlson Architects' design reputation and influenced suburban commercial architecture in Seattle and around the country. Before Larry's, supermarkets were boxy and mundane with little thought toward materials, form, or scale. The architectural massing of Larry's, however, is playful. The materials are ordinary, but used in extraordinary ways. Consequently, suburban buildings sprang up in the region that emulated the forms and materials of Larry's. A sports bar literally copied the Larry's wind vanes and concrete block piers. Larry's was in a national VISA ad. Carlson received calls from architects and developers around the country who wanted to see if Larry would build a store in their area, or to find out the features, costs, materials, and techniques for creating the Larry's architecture. The arts community also appreciated the buildings for the strength and playfulness of the forms, the beauty and durability of the industrial materials, and the quality of the interior lighting.

Kirkland, 1989

Left: A sidewalk café, flower shop, and pavilion-style entry bring life to the store's entrance. Above: Crenelated windows, Y shaped downspouts, and colored metal forms face the nearby interstate freeway interchange. Below: Windows in the café's sawtooth roof flood the interior with day light.

Above left: A simple, yet dramatic gable roof caps Larry's Tukwila store.
Above right: This early sketch explores elements for the Bellevue store.
Below left: The interior of Tukwila's café opens to a sidewalk seating
section. Below right: The assemblage of elements at Larry's Oak Tree
store reduces the overall scale and creates an active sidewalk.

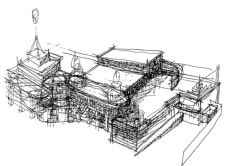

Bellevue, 1990

Above left: Building elements form a gateway at the entrance. Below Left: The exterior of Bellevue Larry's boasts a modern image. Middle: The architects added green glazed block as a new material at Bellevue. Above right: On the interior, a stair with a platform landing leads to administration areas on the second floor. Below right: In response to Bellevue's glass towers, the store's architecture is sleek and horizontal.

Petaluma Factory Outlet

Village Petaluma, California, 1992

The strategy of factory outlet center developments is to cluster factory outlet stores of name brand manufacturers near vacation destinations outside major metropolitan areas. Chelsea Group, the project developer, acquired a site 40 miles north of San Francisco in Petaluma. This small, historic city located on Highway 101 leads to, among other recreational spots, the major wine producing areas of Northern California. Petaluma's history is rooted in agriculture. The town was once known as the "egg basket" of the world. Hatcheries, farm sheds, grain elevators, and vernacular agricultural buildings constructed with industrial materials define the local architectural character.

Chelsea Group's first factory outlet projects were located near tourist areas around New York and New England, which necessitated development sensitive to the traditional towns and architecture. Accordingly, they plan their projects as "villages" consisting of individual shops lining promenades and open spaces. Different than strip malls or quick-trip centers, factory outlets are destinations, where visitors often spend hours exploring and shopping. The straightforward program for Petaluma included 200,000 square feet of flexible retail space for shops and food providers, and parking for 1,000 cars.

The highly visible 25-acre site is above the flood plain situated between Highway 101 and the Petaluma River. The developer's diagram for the village was a simplistic, symmetrical pedestrian loop with shops on each side and a cul-de-sac of shops on each end. The essential design challenge was to disguise this symmetry and add variety to the simple circulation pattern. Carlson decided to create a pedestrian village with diverse spatial experiences, reminiscent of a medieval town, where narrow and twisting walkways open into piazzas with distant views of prominent towers, and hidden courtyards that add a sense of exploration and discovery. The design provided each space along the circulation path with its own identity.

While developing these identities, Carlson examined the open spaces and the buildings along the circulation path. A different identity and name was developed for each open space. Function, physical size, shape, and surrounding greenery helped to define each space: the "X" Square, Fountain Court, Café Square, Oak Park, Fan Plaza, Willow Plaza, and Palm Square. These spaces were landscaped with indigenous trees, grasses, and vines. Corrugated metal cistern fountains and tractor-seat benches refer to Petaluma's agricultural heritage.

Clay drain pipe shaped columns rhythmically line a narrow walk leading to the Willow Plaza.

The architects developed a "kit of parts" consisting of building types and a palette of common materials that could be combined in many variations. The massing and vitality of local agricultural architecture informed these choices. The materials palette consists of galvanized and painted corrugated metal roofing and siding, brick end caps with accent colors and graphics, exposed steel structures, and terra-cotta clay columns. The plaster walls were painted ochre and red—colors that work well in the light of California. Steel canopy columns were designed to hold colorful banners.

Carlson developed a series of three building types—linear buildings, cluster buildings, and landmark buildings. Each building type plays a specific role in shaping the open spaces and creating diversity in the architecture. The linear buildings are long shed-type buildings with rooftop monitors. They are the primary site-organizing buildings. Their configuration ("I," "L," or "T") varies according to the site circulation pattern to be defined. The cluster buildings are composite buildings incorporating a variety of shapes (boxes, sheds, drums, towers) that interlock to create focal points and reduce the scale of façades along the walkways. The landmark buildings are prime location buildings with unique shapes. The architects designed all of the buildings to function as flexible commercial spaces that generate and reinforce the identity of each open space, create focal views, play off of each other, and create a varied scale within the project. The different building types, diverse materials, and animated massing create an intriguing sight that draws people in.

Signage was an integral part of the design. The logo for the center resembles a traditional crate marking. Directories and direction signs, located at entries, orient visitors. The building façades accommodate a sign I.D. system for each store that maintains consistency. A large, linear letter sign mounted on the roof of the center building identifies the factory outlet village to motorists passing on the highway.

Below: Site plan Right: Galvanized metal and landscaping elements create landmarks throughout the village.

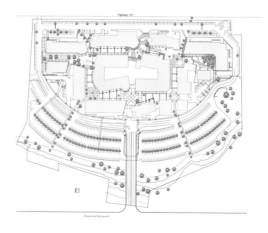

Above left: The food court, with its spacious interior café, is the focal point of Oak Park. Below left: These early sketches explore Petaluma's building elements. Middle: The centerpiece of Willow Plaza features a farm inspired tank and spilling water feature. Above right: The diverse building types create a village feel. Below right: Varied spatial experiences disguise the simple circulation pattern. Far right: Oak Park's food court also features an outdoor café.

Evergreen State College

Olympia, Washington, 1993

Arts Lab Annex

Evergreen State College is a progressive experimental school founded in the 1960s. The campus was carved out of dense evergreen forest near the state capital. The architecture of the original campus consisted solely of austere modern concrete structures. However, as the campus expanded, structures employing a variety of forms and materials have greatly increased the architectural diversity. The arts lab, an original campus building, has been expanded twice to accommodate and consolidate the art programs. The first expansion occurred in the late '80s with the addition of painting studios and a ceramics kiln building.

In 1990, Carlson Architects was awarded the job of adding sculpture facilities to complete the art school consolidation. The program brief called for 10,000 square feet of new and renovated space to house a wood shop, sculpture assembly studio, drawing studio, expanded ceramics studio, metal casting and metal shop, along with outdoor work spaces.

The design created an architecturally unified complex of linked building elements interspersed with outdoor work and gathering spaces. The addition seamlessly reinforces the organization of the existing building, which is a compound of connected but separate individual building elements.

The arts lab is prominently sited on an entry path leading to the center of campus. The site is steep, with forest on the uphill side and campus loading on the downhill side. The addition, sited on the lowest level, consolidates all sculpture facilities on one level and takes advantage of the loading areas. Strategic placement of the new program building elements—wood shop, casting shed, and sculpture assembly studio—completes the "compound" organization of the arts lab. Outdoor work areas, essential for making large sculpture, are located at each end of the assembly studio. A stair, landscaped with low flowering shrubs and trees, connects the new outdoor work areas to outdoor spaces on the level above. The architects located the drawing studio on the lower level with the renovated metal shop, the new wood shop, and the assembly studio. They also expanded the ceramics studio on the uphill second level.

The unique shape of each new building element matches its function. In order to meet fire code regulations, a saw-tooth concrete firewall separates the wood shop from the other building elements. It is echoed by the north-facing saw-tooth skylights of the roof, which provide shadow-free work lighting and minimize the need for artificial light during the day.

A continuous skylight runs along the north-south axis of the building, providing perfect natural light for the sculpture assembly studio.

The casting shed is an open-air structure with a simple, sloped roof for weather protection. The sculpture assembly studio, which functions as a transparent divider between the wood shop and the main structure, has a sloped glass roof that provides strong daylight to the interior. Materials in the addition mirror those of the existing building—cast concrete base, steel frame walls and roof structure, and white painted metal standing seam walls and roofing.

The arts lab complex, with its series of diverse yet similar building elements and multi-level outdoor workspaces, is a constantly changing performance place. The extensions add variety, contrast, and informality to the shapes and materials of the brutal concrete of the existing '60s campus architecture. Walking past the arts lab is a fascinating experience. Wherever one looks, art and the making of art is visible—in each outdoor area, on each level, and through large windows in the ceramics and sculpture studios.

Below left: The sculpture studio additions extend the existing architectural vocabulary of the building. Above: Site plan Below right: North-facing sawtooth skylights provide shadow free light for the woodshop.

Seattle, Washington, 1994,

Seattle

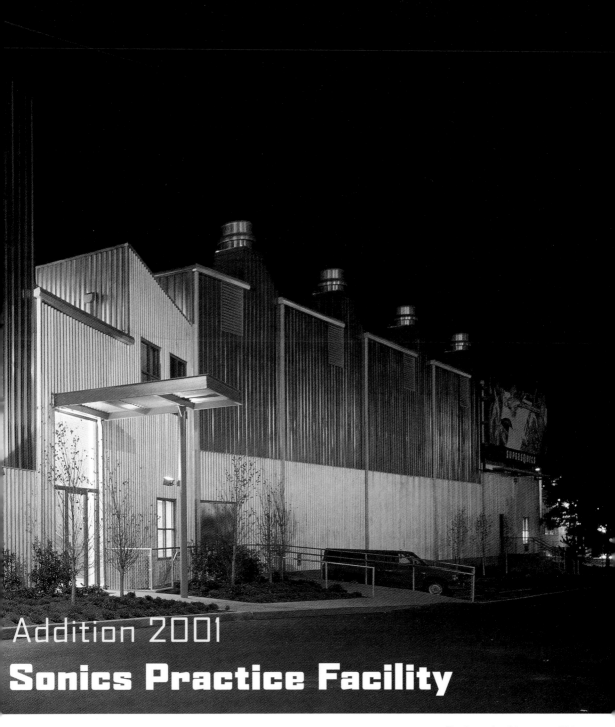

Addition 2001

Sonics Practice Facility

The Ackerley family, which owned the Sonics when the practice facility was designed, also owns a national media company with radio stations and advertising billboards. A 558,000-square-foot site at the Seattle Center, near the arena where the team plays, accommodates the practice facility. Each day, thousands of cars stream by the site at the intersection of Highway 99 and Mercer, a major east-west thoroughfare. The Ackerleys asked Carlson to incorporate strategically placed billboards for team promotion into the design of the building.

The program for the initial 30,000-square-foot facility included two regulation NBA basketball courts, locker rooms, workout and training facilities, offices for administrative personnel and coaching staff, and a lounge with a viewing platform overlooking the courts. In 2000, the Ackerley family made a successful bid for an expansion team in the WNBA, which necessitated expansion of the original facility by 4,200 square feet to provide locker rooms for the women's team plus a new media and press center.

At the time the Sonics franchise was established in Seattle, the Boeing Company was working on the design of the supersonic transport SST. The design concept was to develop an architectural image for the building that would connect the team's name to Seattle's reputation as a center of the aviation industry. In addition, Carlson wanted to animate the inherently "large box" building to capture the attention of motorists on the highway.

With a combination of eccentric shapes, colors, and billboards, the building stands out. The exterior is clad in two ribbed patterns of green and silver metal. Four six-foot exhaust fan housings rhythmically line the edge of the roof, recalling the intakes of jet engines. A green metal-clad elevator "tower," topped by a large communications dish that receives all available sports and news broadcasts via satellite, marks the main entry to the building. A two-story red steel and glass frame splits the building between the elevator shaft and the two-story wing to bring natural light into the entry lobby. A tall, angular red metal box protrudes from the south end of the building like an exclamation point.

The practice courts are housed in a warehouse-type building with a simple shed roof—no natural light was permitted, because the practice sessions had to replicate game conditions. A two-story attachment to the courts contains locker rooms, training facilities, and physical therapy facilities on the first floor, and offices, a lounge, and a spectator viewing area

Above: The combination of eccentric shapes, colors, and details (like the exhaust fans and communications dish) animates this inherently "large box" building type and captures the attention of passing motorists. Below: The highway side acts as a buffer to the entry side of the building.

on the second floor. The lounge, the main gathering place, has a high-bay ceiling with clerestory windows, which flood the space with natural light. The south wing, which houses the Storm's locker rooms, coaches' offices, and training/therapy facilities, is accentuated by an eccentric red metal protrusion with a dramatically tilted roof that provides a media/press space where news conferences are held and reporters interview the team.

The facility is constructed with an exposed steel structure of columns, beams, and trusses. The structure is painted white and illuminated with indirect light from suspended fluorescent fixtures. Exposed recessed can-type fixtures are suspended by cable from the ceiling for additional accent down lighting.

Three billboards attached to jutting building elements continually rotate promotional images, which reinforces the "high speed" architecture of the facility.

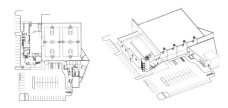

Above left: Site/floor plan Above right: Axonometric drawing Below left:
These early sketches explore the building's massing. Below middle:
Bright red canopies protrude over the eight-foot doors, sized to accommodate the seven-foot players. Below right: The tilted plane of the red-
clad media room peaks at 30 feet, giving the room a dramatic feeling
inside and a strong presence from the highway.

Above: Lighting in the two full-sized courts is carefully balanced to provide the exact conditions found in the team's home arena. Above right: Continuing the industrial aesthetic, the exposed ceilings were painted white and up lit to create a tall spacious feeling throughout. Below right: The therapy pool is eight feet deep for rehab exercising.

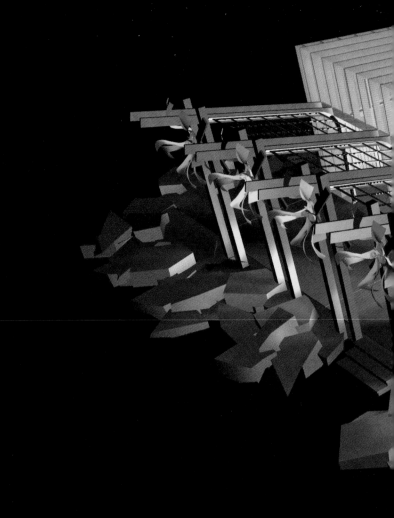

Kobe Community Centers

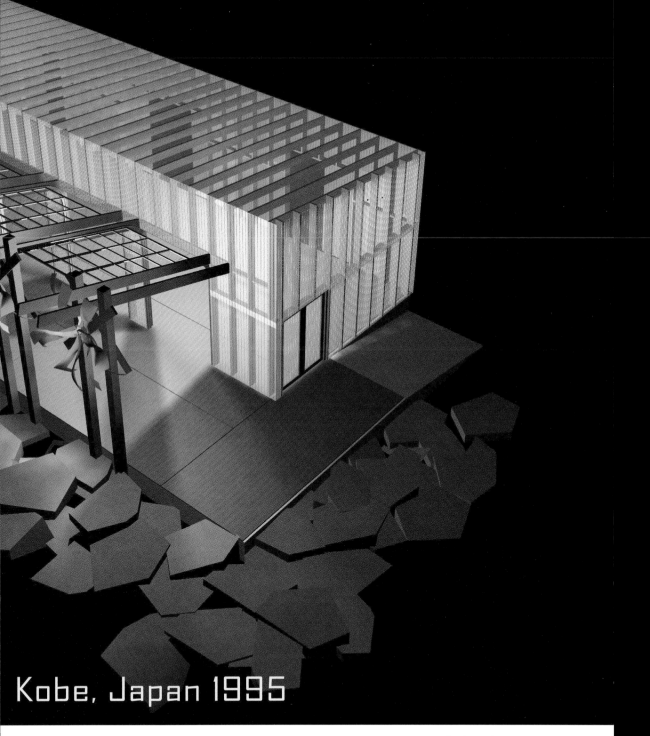

Kobe, Japan 1995

The Great Hanshin Earthquake of January 17, 1995, left hundreds of thousands of people in the city of Kobe and surrounding areas without housing. Earthquake survivors were also left without gathering places where they could come together as a community. While local and national governments embarked on plans to provide interim and permanent replacement housing, the International Council of AIA Seattle decided to target the problem of providing community meeting places for Kobe. The Council mounted an architectural competition to provide a design that would quickly respond to the needs of the Kobe citizenry. The simple program called for 1,200 square feet of flexible temporary space for community meetings and social activities. The entries were judged upon ease of transport and erection, adaptability, and use of materials. The Council preferred a design that made use of Washington State products, and provided emotional and spiritual benefits for the community. The jury sought design solutions expressing and furthering the relationships between Washington State and the Hyogo Prefecture, and sister cities Kobe and Seattle. State agencies, businesses, groups, and individuals pledged materials, time, and money to provide ten to 20 shelters.

Carlson Architects' winning design was dubbed the "community living room." The simple, flexible building opens up like a flower for large gatherings or closes for smaller events. Although the basic structure would be the same for each unit, each neighborhood could personalize its building with decorations and embellishments, making them familiar, welcoming, and spiritual. The architects chose materials that evoked a warm, glowing lantern. The jurors cited the Carlson design as "poetic….elemental, and economical," and commended "a delightful experience day or night" with apparent simplicity and cost-effectiveness.

The individual building is a simple pavilion—a large open room 20 feet wide by 60 feet long by 16 feet high. The pavilion is surrounded on three sides by a platform that serves as a porch and expands the domain of the 1,200-square-foot enclosure. Five wood and glass garage doors, eight feet wide by ten feet tall, roll up and out over the porch to provide a canopy-like cover that allows smooth circulation through the pavilion during large events. Six "totemic" double columns lining the porch serve as supports for the rolling door tracks, and provide a place for embellishment and individual identity. The porch perimeter is edged with remnants of buildings toppled by the earthquake. Brick panels, rock, pillars, stair sections, and rubble provide places for sitting and also evoke memory, reflection, and hope.

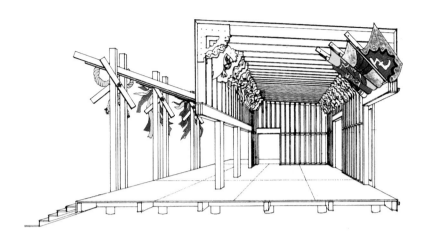

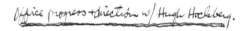

Office progress + direction w/ Hugh Hochberg.

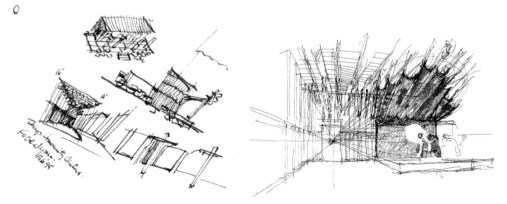

Above: The luminous glow of the space and the rhythm of the wood structure create a simple elegance, while fanciful plywood gussets add color and liveliness to the structural frame. Below left and right: These sketches explore the experiential qualities of both the interior and exterior of the structure.

The rear side of the pavilion is the working side and functions similarly to a warehouse loading dock or the backstage of a theater. Three large dock-high openings, with large side-rolling doors, allow trucks containing support and auxiliary items to "plug" into the pavilion like life support systems. Toilets, catered foods, arts and crafts, and even mobile performance trucks can be attached to provide live theater, dance, and puppet shows.

The pavilion uses utilitarian wood frame construction. Simple foundation blocks support the "pallet" panels, which are recycled from pallets used in shipping the pre-assembled pieces from Seattle to Kobe. The wood frame is exposed on the interior. The structural members of the wall and ceiling are tied together with plywood gusset plates cut in symbolic silhouettes to depict Japanese cultural symbols, such as Kabuki masks and flowers. Colorful stains are used to differentiate building parts, designate order of assembly, and enliven the interior.

The pavilion acts as a thin "membrane" that shelters and provides a backdrop for human activities. Incandescent exposed light bulbs on dimmer switches are socket mounted at the top of the long walls between the colorful gusset plates to provide ambient light for the interior. The roof, walls, and sliding loading doors are clad with translucent corrugated fiberglass panels. The translucent skin allows natural light to softly illuminate the pavilion interior by day and creates a lantern-like glow at night.

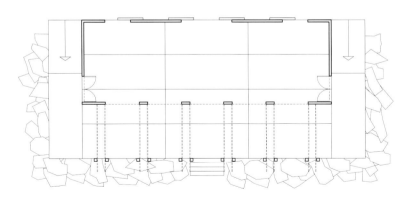

Above: Floor plan Right: The glowing pavilion symbolizes hope for the community, while implying both the fragility and durability of life.

Timberland North Mason

Belfair, Washington, 1998

Public Library

Belfair is a small town in Timberland North Mason County that grew as a linear strip along a rural highway carved out of the dense evergreen forest of the Olympic Peninsula. Historically, the economy of the area was dominated by the timber industry. Sawmill sheds and compounds were the most prominent local architecture. However, over the years the mills disappeared, leaving Belfair with nondescript and conventional commercial buildings. The new public library provides Belfair with a meaningful civic architectural image.

The new 15,000-square-foot library, which is designed to hold 75,000 books, replaced a 3,500-square-foot facility that no longer met the needs of the community. The site, located on highway 3, the main street of Belfair, is heavily wooded and backs up to a dense wetland forest that extends to nearby Hood Canal. Rather than demolish the existing library, the architects chain-sawed it into three separate sections, which they barged down Hood Canal and reassembled to provide a new library for the small town of Hoodsport.

The new library is a civic landmark that reflects the timbering heritage of Belfair. Carlson designed a building that is "in and of the forest." The structure was carved into the site, which preserved the maximum number of mature firs and cedars. It is set back from the road and, at night, light from the interior is visible in the large windows and clerestory. A marker sign constructed with similar materials as the building indicates the entrance. A curved entry road winds through the trees, past the building entry and into the 67-car parking lot. From there the main entry, in the central spine of the building, is directly accessible.

Simple exterior materials, such as concrete block and ribbed metal wall and roof cladding, recall local mill building construction. However, variations in material, color, and texture reinforce the "building in the forest" design concept. Black split-face concrete block and dark green metal roofs allow the building to recede into the forest like tree trunks or dark shadows. Weathered silver galvanized metal cladding on the spine roof and main reading room walls glistens in the light, calling attention to the library.

The building's organization resembles a tightly knit compound with separate building elements that are linked by a tall central circulation spine. The separate components include the main reading room, the children's library and meeting room, and the staff work area. The spine is reminiscent of a mill-run shed. The plywood ceilings leave their mill stamp

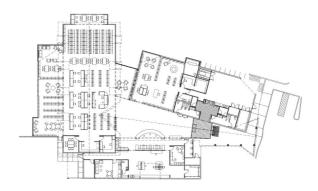

Left: Floor plan Above: The diagonal entry spine connects all areas of the library, dramatically rising to the skylight above the main reading room. An arched opening made with wood slats allows visibility into the children's area.

"tattoos" exposed as signatures of the industry. Large timber trusses support the roof of the circulation spine and the main reading room, and high clerestory windows allow natural light in, giving the impression of an open air shed. The ridge of the spine ascends to its apex at the junction of the main reading room, where a large triangular skylight brings daylight into the heart of the library. The architects designed the skylight as a forest canopy of layered branches. They overlaid the joining roof frames, extended the rafter tails, and supplemented the structure with additional members to create a trellis-like baffle that filters and deflects the sunlight as it falls into the space.

The design orients interior spaces to the surrounding wetland forest. The staff area is located on the street side of the building and provides a buffer for the public areas. The staff area includes a staff lounge, large workroom, and librarian's office, and a loading area on the south end. The staff area is directly behind the circulation desk, which is located just inside the front door and has clear sight lines to all areas of the library. Large windows in sitting and reading areas provide tranquil views deep into the forest. Other windows, high above the roofline, heighten the forest views and offer craning glimpses into tree canopies. A large window at the end of the main reading room protrudes into the forest domain. Visitors enter the children's area through a spire-shaped doorway in a slatted wood frame wall. A mysterious stick-tree-framed opening beckons children into the story telling nook—a glass room looking into the forest.

Light fixtures throughout the library contribute to the "forest" building metaphor. Industrial fixtures are fitted with custom mountings for both direct and indirect lighting. Exposed flexible conduit connects the fixtures and twines around light brackets like vines twisting to the light. In the children's area, standard fluorescent light fixtures hung playfully from the ceiling at random heights and angles create an underwater effect.

Above: Section throught the spine Right: Daylight pours through a skylight and continuous clerestory windows running the length of the spine. Far right: A large bay window at the end of the main reading room offers a panoramic view deep into the forest.

Left and middle: Custom designed lights using industrial fixtures provide both direct and indirect lighting, while invigorating the interior as sculptural elements. Right: The roof structure rises in a corner reading area to heighten the forest view. Far right: The intersection of the building structures at the central skylight creates a trellis-like effect that baffles sunlight entering the space.

University of Washington

Seattle, Washington, 1999
School of Social Work Addition

When the School of Social Work building was constructed in 1979, only two of the three planned stories were built due to budget constraints. From the beginning, the building was considered sterile and fortress-like. It did not represent the people-oriented attitude of the school. The building was also dark inside; offices had narrow strip windows and classrooms didn't have any windows at all. Twenty years later, money was appropriated for a 10,000-square-foot addition. Carlson Architects promised to design an addition that was inspirational and not institutional.

In addition to not representing the attitude of the school, the building was too small. The School of Social Work was renting nearby office space, as well as additional space for the many conferences, seminars, and workshops they sponsor. Accordingly, the program called for a multi-purpose room and support spaces, new faculty offices, and classroom/break-out rooms.

The building is located between the Gothic university campus and "The Ave"—a gritty commercial street lined with small shops and cafes. The transitional location allowed the architecture to evoke the school's progressive philosophy and programs without the constraints of campus precedent and tradition. It could have its own character and personality—be more flamboyant and gregarious—to relate more to the commercial district and the community, just as the School of Social Work reaches out to the community. The space available for the expansion was the portion of the roof originally intended for a third floor plus the setback area between the south end of the building and the adjacent street.

The architects created an animated addition that contrasts with the monolithic original building. The design concept defined the existing building as the "site" for the new addition—a "mesa" or "plateau" on which the addition would be built. The designers located the multi-purpose room, classrooms, and circulation areas on the roof. Faculty offices, new lobbies, and a new elevator vertically clad the south end of the building.

The resulting penthouse addition forms a new profile for the building with a series of connected individually shaped building elements that appear as a rooftop village. The addition is necessarily lightweight to minimize the structural loading on the existing building. A steel frame and cladding of ribbed metal panels were used. The metal cladding is either galvanized silver gray or copper green, which reinforces the appearance of individual building elements.

Right: A dramatic office tower and curved lobby sit atop an extended brick podium and stair, designed to match the original building.

The new metal-clad forms extend over the south end of the building with new lobbies at each floor. A three-story stack of faculty offices creates a prominent landmark tower on the end of the building. The base of the existing building is extended in matching brick to form an elevated platform on which the office tower rests. A new entry stair angles up from the busiest pedestrian corner to allow direct access to the building's main floor above. The stair also provides a sunny, social sitting area.

The interior spaces reflect the roof volumes and the form of the building elements. The intersection of individual building elements with the interior volumes is unexpected and sculptural. The structure is exposed except where the architects installed sound insulation between structural members. The interior hallway circuitously winds from volume to volume. All common spaces are social spaces—lobbies, nooks, corridors, and rooftop decks are designed to promote informal discussions. Interior color is mostly off-white so the volumes read. The architects used dark and medium green to provide accent and further define the architecture. Fluorescent uplights wash the structure and ceilings, highlighting the interior volumes. Built-in wood benches for informal conversations and study inhabit strategic corners. A fluorescent fixture mounted diagonally out from the wall above each bench provides light on the seating area. Unlike the original building, the addition is filled with natural light. Roof forms lift up to create clerestory windows that allow natural light to enter over each multi-purpose room entry. Large windows throughout the addition frame views of the campus, distant mountains, and the city. The south-facing lobby windows aim directly at Mount Rainier.

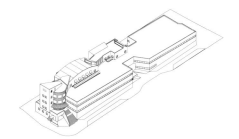

Left: Shape and color define individual elements that form a varied building "skyline." Middle: New gathering spaces on each floor of the rounded tower element offer views of the campus and Mt. Rainier in the distance. Right: The bowed ceiling of the multi-purpose room creates an open atmosphere, while the windows offer distant views. Above: Axonometric drawing.

Seattle, Washington, 1997
Carlson House

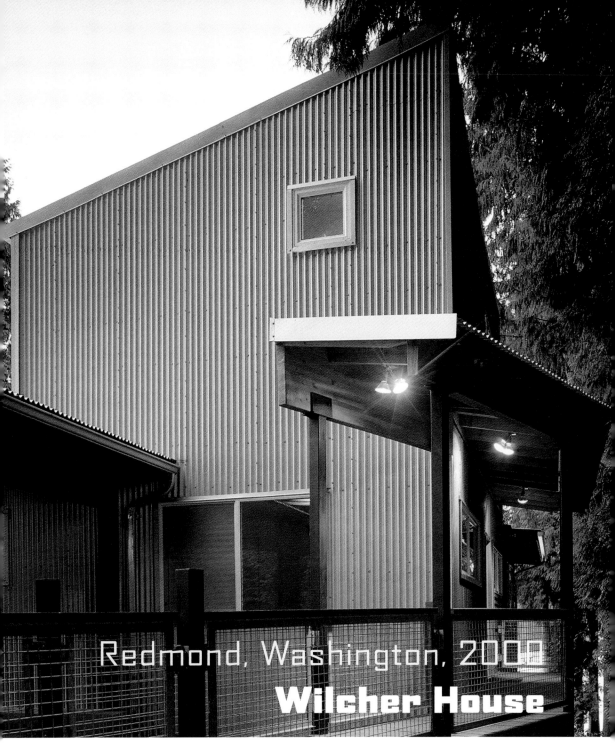

Redmond, Washington, 2000
Wilcher House

Carlson Architects used two projects, the Carlson house and the Wilcher house, to experiment with the idea of converting existing houses into loft living environments. Though each house was located on a spectacular site, they were conventional buildings and had no redeeming architectural merit. The architects designed the projects sequentially, incorporating variations on the loft house concept.

The design reorganized interior and exterior spaces to create playful, open, light-filled dwellings that capitalize on the site and views. Building elements added to the basic box houses changed the exterior appearance and gave each house a distinctive architectural presence. The architects explored the use of unconventional materials, the contrast of new to existing, the vertical penetration of light shafts, the use of structural frames as sculptural elements, and the use of inexpensive fixtures to achieve dramatic lighting effects.

The Carlson house features a metal clad loft box, which is notched into the side. A second floor tower, housing the master bedroom, bath, and central stair, and a floating roof plane over the back deck animate the Wilcher house. Walls of the existing houses were darkened—the Carlson house with black asphalt shingles, the Wilcher with deep charcoal green paint. The architects used silver corrugated metal as the dominant new material for the roofs and additions. The result is an architecturally diverse structure with both receding and glowing building elements.

The existing entries, located against the neighboring driveway, provided no sense of passage or ceremony. Each new entry solution captures the essence of the site. At Carlson, the entry walk, which proceeds along the south side next to a long garden, has a view of Lake Washington and the Cascade Mountains, framed by the exposed structure of the loft box. Rainwater from the roof falls from a gutter spout above and splashes into a "cattle tank" near the entry door. At Wilcher, a new steel and wood dock-like walkway winds around the corner of the house, alongside a neighboring evergreen forest, to reveal a view out to Ames Lake.

The most dramatic changes occur on the inside, where each house opens up horizontally and vertically to create spacious flowing interiors. The architects gutted the Carlson house to the frame and only rebuilt the interior walls surrounding two bathrooms. It is a "raw" exploration of the contrast between new finishes and the existing building structure— exposed gang-nail trusses and plywood roof decking add intricacy and heighten the space. The archi-

Carlson House
Above: The metal-clad box addition floats over the new entry, while the garden room and deck addition extend from the rear of the house. Left: Concealed spotlights above wash through the steel grating of the stairs and plant shelf to create dramatic shadow patterns. Right: Wiring for the exposed canlights is wound around plumbing pipes. Switched outlets mounted in the ceiling allow lights to be clipped anywhere. Lights in the pantry reveal items behind the perforated corrugated metal door panels.

tects cut a large opening between the two main levels and left a few floor joists intact to support an isolated reading "perch" in the corner. All levels are interconnected—stairs lead to the second level, a steel stair ascends to the loft box, and a ladder climbs through a roof hatch to the topmost roof deck, where a large skylight brings natural light all the way back down through the house.

The Wilcher house also features a light shaft carved through three stories, starting with a south-facing clerestory window at the new upper master bedroom level, extending through the main living level and ending down at the daylight basement level. The architects peeled away the flooring at the first level to expose the floor structure and allow sunlight to filter into the space. Exposed structural wood frame walls clad with wood slats create moving studies of light and shadow in the light shafts. Both houses have simple plywood flooring (white ash and maple), secured with exposed fasteners.

Lighting is the final layer in the composition. Simple and inexpensive fixtures such as strip fluorescent lights, exterior spotlight mounts, porcelain sockets, and exposed recessed-type can lights achieved dramatic effects. In the Carlson house, recessed can lights, mounted upside-down to the side of an exposed linear mechanical duct, wash the trusses and roof deck with soft indirect light. Spotlight mounts concealed in an upper loft recess cast strong light through the open grating stairs of the steel bridge and make shadow patterns on the entry wall. Porcelain mounts with exposed bulbs backlight a closet wall of rolling doors clad in corrugated fiberglass, causing them to glow. In the central light well of the Wilcher house, concealed spotlight mounts wash the wood structure with dramatic light. Suspended light tracks float at varying angles below the slightly pitched ceiling in the main living space. A triangular hole cut in the drywall ceiling of the bedroom reveals the floor structure. A warped punched silver metal shield suspended under the hole hides a dimmable bare incandescent bulb mounted in a porcelain socket in the recess. Light reflects back up on the ceiling and passes through the punched metal in a delightful play.

Carlson House
Left: Main floor plan Above: The open second floor makes the small house feel spacious. Below: Daylight from a window penetrates the translucent fiberglass rolling door panels of the closet. Right: A steel stair rises four feet to the loft bedroom. In the far corner, a reading area floats over the living room below.

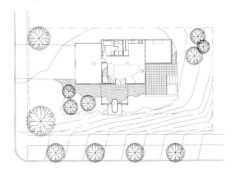

Wilcher House

Left: The sloped roof canopy appears to be a floating plane, while silver elements define the addition from the lake. Middle: The interior of the small existing house was cleaned out and opened up to achieve a sense of spaciousness. Plywood panels clad the floor. Right: The central light shaft is permeated by light from a south-facing window.

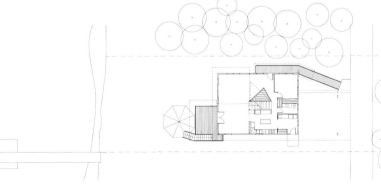

Wilcher House
Left and middle: Viewed from below and from the main level, the central
light shaft illustrates the sculptural effect created by the criss-crossing
layers of wood structure and slats. Right: The master bedroom, located
on the top level, offers panoramic views of Lake Ames and the adjacent
fir forest. Below: Main level plan

Bellwether Buildings

Bellingham, Washington, 2001

Like many coastal cities in the Pacific Northwest, Bellingham's waterfront developed with industries related to fishing and timber resources. Over time, the importance of these resource industries diminished and the Port of Bellingham began looking to recreational boating and tourism facilities as appropriate waterfront uses. In the early 1980s the Port doubled the size of their existing marina by dredging tidal mudflats and creating an upland peninsula with the dredged material. Over the ensuing 15 years, development on the peninsula was limited to a restaurant and small Coast Guard station. In the late 1990s, the Port initiated a development program that aimed at fully utilizing this unique waterfront property.

The Port hired Carlson Architects to develop a master plan to guide development of the peninsula. A central road and sidewalks were put in 20 years ago as part of the original development. The narrow peninsula and central road resulted in linear potential building parcels. The challenge was to create a plan that would be more spatially diverse, rather than a simple row of narrow buildings lining a street, while at the same time maintaining the existing infrastructure. The resulting plan creates a cluster of buildings surrounding a public "town square" and adjacent waterfront park. The square and park are programmed for live music concerts and other community events during summer months. The design provides pedestrian access around the perimeter of the peninsula and allows visitors views of the marina, Bellingham Bay, the San Juan Islands, and the surrounding community. The new buildings include a small hotel and two high tech office buildings with retail space on the first level. The square and cluster of new buildings sit atop a half-underground, 300-car parking structure, allowing for optimum utilization of the land area and creating a sense of "topography" at the end of the otherwise flat peninsula. Each of the new buildings can be accessed directly from the parking garage. The square features large glass block inserts that allow natural light into the garage during the day and a warm glow into the square at night.

The Port retained Carlson to design the two mixed-use buildings. The character of the working waterfront influenced Carlson's design. The simple gable roof forms and open shed canopies recall the shapes of fish processing warehouses and fishing net sheds. In both buildings, the use of ground-face concrete block and zinc roof and wall panels suggests the simplicity of industrial structures. Large sculptural steel members, reminiscent of davits,

Above: The port building forms the edge of the public plaza. Cast iron ship moorings define the drive that crosses the plaza. Right: A bending covered walkway and rhythmic colonnade define the building's marina side entry.

the small cranes on ships' sides used in hoisting boats and stores, dramatically define the perimeter of the square and provide supports for sheltering canopies.

The buildings bend at various angles, creating multiple façades and views in all directions. This design reinforces the master plan by creating frontages that frame the open spaces. Each building plays a role in the composition of the "village" cluster. The larger 43,500-square-foot building is the dominant façade on the square. A prominent zinc-clad stair tower faces the main roadway and marks the entry to the square. The architects angled the building to face the square and main entry road. Where the structure bends, a public passageway through the building provides direct access to the square.

The smaller 34,000-square-foot structure also forms an edge to the larger public square and wraps around its own smaller plaza. The centerpiece of the small plaza is a steel and glass pavilion with a roof curved in the shape of a seashell.

The plaza pavilion (shown here before glazing) is a sculptural combination of two shapes—a floating curved roof plane and a metal clad "solid" that contains support space.

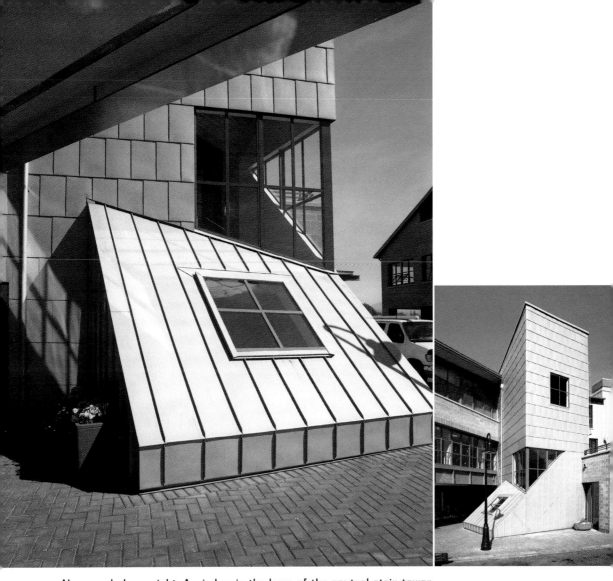

Above and above right: A window in the base of the central stair tower admits light to the parking garage stair and glows at night, while windows in the tower above provide views of the plaza and bay.

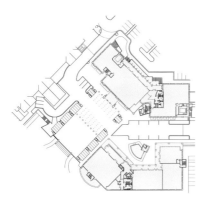

Left: Castellated beams and extended purlin tails add scale and dimension to the steel structure of the canopy. Middle: Inside the central stair tower, winding stairs, metal cladding, a view of Bellingham Bay, and a custom buoy light creates a more interesting route upstairs than taking the elevator. Right: Sunsets highlight the two-story curved metal shingle wall in the lobby. Above: The partial site plan illustrates the relationship of the jointed buildings and the exterior spaces they frame.

Ballard Lofts Seattle

Washington, 2001

The Ballard area of Seattle has a long and proud history related to fishing, shipbuilding, and ship repair. The city is located on Salmon Bay, which is lined with gritty marine-related industrial buildings and piers. A busy drawbridge spans the ship canal on Salmon Bay, connecting Ballard to downtown Seattle. The Ballard Lofts is prominently located adjacent to the north end of the bridge and a block away from the waterfront, on a site previously used for surface parking.

The unique waterfront character of the area is attractive to new businesses, especially the technology community, for its industrial heritage and proximity to downtown. The client saw an opportunity to develop a building that would mix new high-tech uses with the still-viable marine uses of old Ballard. The program called for flexible open space to accommodate the varied uses with street-related light industrial and limited retail space planned for the ground floor.

Carlson's design concept was to create a modern loft building that would have the flexibility, openness, and raw beauty of a traditional industrial loft structure. In addition, the architects intended the building to complement the gritty, industrial character of the neighborhood both in form and materials.

Ballard Lofts is a four-story, 72,000-square-foot structure. The building wraps around the corner site in an L-shaped configuration, creating two wings. A prow-like tower, housing the main entry, stairway, and other core elements, anchors the corner at the turn of the "L." The tower slants out to create a landmark element, identifying the building at the busy street intersection and from the bridge. The architects sited the building to front the adjacent streets, enhancing its presence, visibility, and urban function. On the inside of the "L," the wings of the building frame a parking area. The architects took advantage of the sloping site by designing an inconspicuous two-level structure, consisting of an upper parking deck located over a lower level of covered parking, both of which offer direct access to the building.

The exterior materials of the building relate to the industrial context of the neighborhood. Walls are constructed of cast concrete at the base, which transitions into a steel frame clad in corrugated metal siding above. The economical, maintenance-free siding is manufactured in long sheets that are secured to the building. Steel canopies and large industrial windows complete the loft building appearance. The designers clad the corner tower in large, black, dia-

Above: The basic rectangular massing is scaled down and modulated by contrasting windows, metal textures, and colors that define building elements. The leaning black stair tower dominates the street corner at the main entry providing further accent. Below: These concept sketches explore the initial building block transitions and joinery.

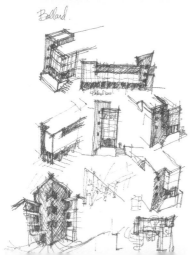

Ballard.

mond-shaped metal shingles, punctuated by slit windows cut into the leading edge of the prow.

The color scheme for the metal siding and the windows "flip-flops" from one side of the building to the other. On the street side, the metal walls are silver with deep red windows and trim; on the parking side, the colors reverse to deep red walls with silver windows and trim. The technique of reversing the colors creates a visual transition on the ends of the building, where the colors and building forms come together. The building elements interlock, notch, and slide by each other in a color-coded joinery that couples the opposite sides of the building.

On the interior, the tower stair winds up past each level to the roof, where a skylight allows natural light and long stair shadows to wind back down. The architects located core elements, such as the elevator, toilets, and shafts, adjacent to the stair to free up each wing for tenant space. Tenanting the building is like outfitting an existing warehouse loft. The high ceilings remain open, exposing the lacey steel frame structure and allowing for vertical flexibility. Large windows and narrow yet open floor plans let natural light deep into the interior space, creating a loft feeling and function. The flexible space can be easily adapted: an entire floor can be left open or subdivided into small spaces with a corridor.

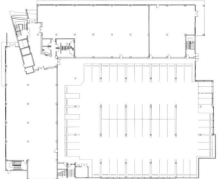

Left: A two level parking structure nestles inside the "L" shaped building, presenting the street with a simple steel frame edge clad with chain link mesh that provides security and transparency. Below: Street level plan Right: Contrasting elements overlap at the ends of the "L" shaped building.

University

Seattle, Washington, 2003
Child Development School

The University Child Development School is a progressive elementary and pre-elementary school with an experiential approach to learning. It has evolved over the years into a prominent, nationally known program. Educators from across the nation come visit the school to observe the learning techniques. The early elementary program actually had its roots in the Reggio Emilia system developed in Italy, which is very exploratory and creative. The individual learning style of each child is nurtured to develop intellect and curiosity. Curriculums each year are developed around a common theme, which provides an interactive focus for learning. Teachers don't lecture; instead, they assist the children as they work individually or in groups on projects that involve exploration of interrelated subjects and skills. Every space in the school is a learning space constantly in use—stairs and hallways become places for quiet reading, discussions, and experimentation. Carlson Architects was selected to design an addition to the existing school that would represent the school's philosophy, support their learning methods, and expand their educational capabilities.

The elementary school occupies a brick building built in 1949, which was formerly a school for a Catholic cathedral located across the street. The European-style cathedral is an impressive neighboring edifice with an ornate brick façade, tall copper spire, and a monumental entry stair. The school is situated between a quiet residential street and a busy commercial one, with a 25-foot difference in elevation between the two streets. The pre-elementary school is currently located in another part of the city.

The purpose of the expansion is to combine both of the school's programs together on one campus and to provide advanced new facilities that enhance the learning process. Interaction among all students and faculty is also a primary goal. The expansion will enable the school to enrich the curriculum by expanding the arts, science, and technology facilities. The expansion program includes administrative spaces, a visiting artist's studio, classrooms, and a discovery area for early elementary school students, as well as a multi-purpose room, library, and other specialized spaces used by both levels.

Carlson's conceptual approach is to create architecturally distinctive, playful elements that blend and contrast with the existing rectilinear brick building, and that illustrate the unique and progressive attitude of the school.

The program is organized on three levels with early elemen-

Above: The design concept for the addition is to complement the existing 1949 building with two new rectilinear brick structures, and then to link them with a contrasting organic metal-clad structure that climbs up the hill. Below: A new entry courtyard and garden visually connect the front façades of both new and old buildings. Below right: These early sketches explore the pitches and angles of the metal addition.

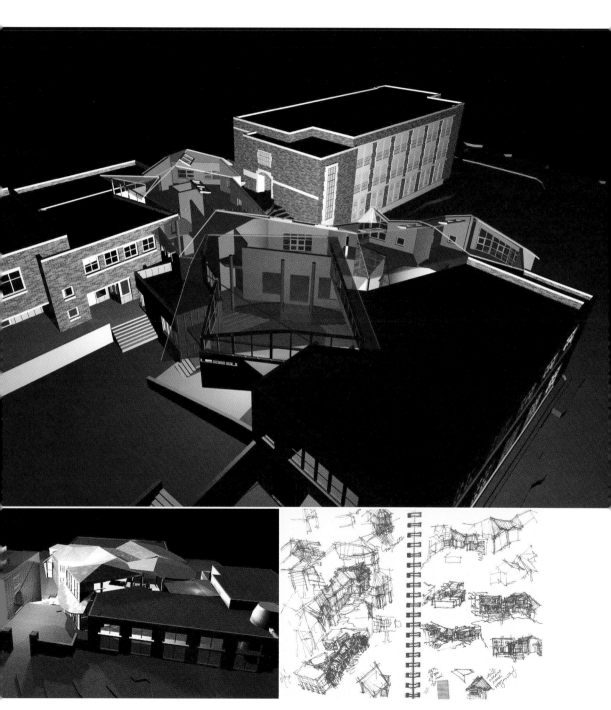

tary, library, and art on the main level, administration and technology on the upper level, and the multipurpose functions on the lower level. The program is also clustered into three distinct building elements. The new brick buildings, which complement the existing building in color and proportion, are located on each street front, and are linked by an angular, metal-clad connector element. Windows and fenestration are proportionate to the old building. The metal building element moves in continuous pitches and angles that make the building appear to curl as it climbs up the hill.

The new building responds to the urban street edge, and shapes outdoor spaces and playgrounds. The main entry, defined by the school "gate" and a new garden courtyard, forms a symbolic social place connecting the entries of each building. From the entry court, a grand outdoor staircase descends to a landing and then down to the main playground. The stair and landing create an amphitheater for events, classes, projects, and impromptu gatherings. The playground has direct access to the multi-purpose room on the lower level.

The interior of the addition is a spatially rich sequence of interconnected spaces that add to the sense of exploration and discovery for the children. All three levels are visually and functionally tied together by a variety of open stairways, bridges, multi-use ramps, angular roofs, and natural light. The designers placed skylights and clerestory windows strategically within the roof system to provide natural light and to make children aware of lighting effects and the movement of the sun. Bright colors accentuate the most sculptural elements. The early elementary program is located in a separate wing under the angular roof structure. Each early elementary space—classrooms and central discovery area—is uniquely shaped and connected by whimsical passage doors. The angular timber skeleton of the building structure is exposed, adding to the openness and playfulness of the interior spaces.

Below left: Bright light from a glass "chimney," which also acts as a ventilation shaft, pulling fresh air through the early elementary wing, washes the translucent fiberglass panels of the "kiva," turning it into a naturally illuminated lampshade. Above: The garden stair between the existing building and the addition creates an intimate enclosing space for outdoor classes and performances. Below right: A colorful bridge spans the passage to the early elementary wing.

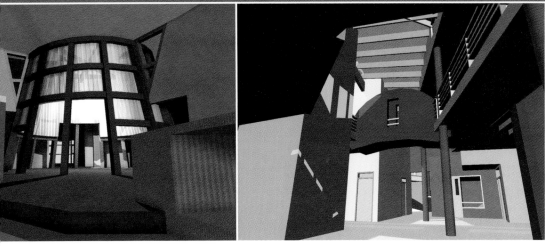

Above: The "discovery" area roof floats above a line of clerestory windows. As the roof structures frame over each other, rafter tails extend out to become an indoor trellis. Below: Floor plans Above right: The visiting artists studio forms the centerpiece to the naturally lit, two story central common area, where gatherings occur and student artwork is shown. Below right: Upon entering the building, spaces flow in all directions.

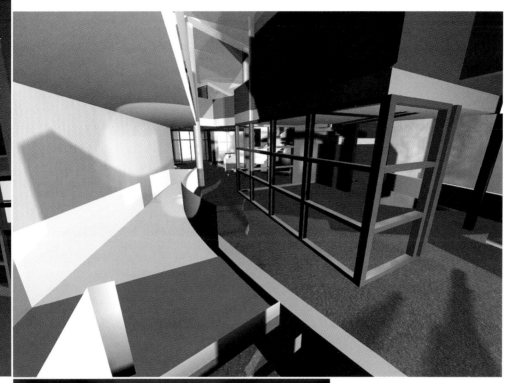

Ballard Lofts Building
Seattle, Washington 2001

Design Team:
Donald E. Carlson, FAIA
Oshien Chen
Mark Withrow
Erin Doherty
Michael Henricks
Eileen McHugh
Marc Roehrle
Andrew Russin

Consultants:
Structural Engineer:
Engineers Northwest

Mechanical Engineer:
Holaday-Parks, Inc.

Electrical Engineer:
Seatac Electric, Inc.

Civil Engineer:
Poggemeyer Design Group

General Contractor:
Foushee & Associates

Surveyor:
Hallin & Associates

Cost Estimator:
Foushee & Associates

Client:
Mastro Properties/Anastasiou
Development

Photography:
Michael Shopenn

Bellwether Office Building
Bellingham, Washington 2001

Design Team:
Donald E. Carlson, FAIA
Scott Hopkins
Paul Whitehill
Oshien Chen
Elisabetta Petronilla Conti

Consultants:
Structural Engineer:
Geiger Engineers

Mechanical Engineer:
Sider & Byers Associates

Electrical Engineer:
Casne Engineering, Inc.

Civil Engineer:
APC Inc.

General Contractor:
Colacurcio Brothers Inc.
Landscape Architect
Hough Beck & Baird

Cost Estimator:
Robinson Company

Client:
Port of Bellingham

Photography:
Rod del Pozo

Carlson Residence
Seattle, Washington 1998

Design Team:
Donald E. Carlson, FAIA
Taka Soga

Consultants:
Structural Engineer:
Swenson Say Faget

General Contractor:
Riewald Construction

Client:
Donald & Donna Carlson

Photography:
Fred Housel
Gregg Krogstad

Evergreen State College
Arts Lab Annex
Olympia, Washington 1993

Design Team:
Donald E. Carlson, FAIA
Allan Ferrin
Kevin Kane

Consultants:
Structural Engineer:
RSP/EQE, Inc.

Mechanical Engineer:
Consulting Design Inc.

Electrical Engineer:
Travis, Fitzmaurice &
Associates

General Contractor:
Jones & Roberts Company

Acoustical Engineer:
Michael Yantis Associates

Lighting Design:
Loveland Millet Lighting Design

Client:
State of Washington
The Evergreen State College

Photography:
Fred Housel

Kobe Community Center
Design Competition
Kobe, Japan 1995

Design Team:
Donald E. Carlson, FAIA
Tom Morris

Client:
Washington State Department
of Economic Development

Larry's Markets
Various locations, Puget
Sound Region, Washington
1986-1992

Design Team:
Donald E. Carlson, FAIA
Hal Eden
Allan Ferrin
Kevin Kane
Terre Meinershagen
Tom Morris
Gail Wong

Consultants:
Structural Engineer:
Engineers Northwest

Mechanical Engineer:
RECO, Inc.

Electrical Engineer:
O'Neill/Stephan Engineers, Inc.

Civil Engineer:
Anne Symonds & Associates

General Contractor:
R.G. Leary, Inc.

Sculptures:
Buster Simpson
(Kirkland Windvanes)

Landscape Architect:
Hugh Beck & Baird

Interior Design:
Suzi McKinney Design

Client:
Larry's Markets
Larry McKinney

Photography:
Fred Housel
Michael Shopenn

Credits

North Mason Timberland Library
Belfair, Washington 1997

Design Team:
Donald E. Carlson, FAIA
Mark Withrow
Jim Hanford
Jamal Salem
Taka Soga

Associate Architect:
Mark Nelson, Library Planning

Consultants:
Structural Engineer:
Swenson Say Faget

Mechanical Engineer:
Sider & Byers Associates

Electrical Engineer:
Hargis Engineering

Civil Engineer:
Bush Roed & Hitchings

General Contractor:
Merit Construction

Landscape Architect:
Hough Beck & Baird

Cost Estimator:
Robinson Company

Client:
Timberland Regional
Library System

Photography:
Fred Housel
Gregg Krogstad

Petaluma Factory Outlet Village
Petaluma California 1992

Design Team:
Donald E. Carlson, FAIA
Allan Ferrin
Hal Eden

Consultants:
Structural Engineer:
RSP/EQE, Inc.

Mechanical Engineer:
Guthrie & Associates

Electrical Engineer:
Hallis Engineering

Civil Engineer:
CSW/Stuber-Stroh Engineering

General Contractor:
Majors Construction

Landscape Architect:
ZAC Landscape Architects

Client:
Chelsea/GCA Realty
Photography:
Todd Pickering

Seattle Supersonics
Practice Facility
Seattle, Washington 1994

Design Team:
Donald E. Carlson, FAIA
Mark Withrow
Dan Umbach
Andrew Russin
Hal Eden

Consultants:
Structural Engineer:
Skilling Ward Magnusson
Barkshire

Mechanical Engineer:
McDonald-Miller Company

Electrical Engineer:
Hooper Electric
Sequoyah Electric

Civil Engineer:
KPFF Engineering
Skilling Ward Magnusson
Barkshire

General Contractor:
Bayley Construction
Turner Contstruction

Landscape Architect:
Hough Beck & Baird

Cost Estimator:
Bayley Construction
Robinson Company

Client:
Seattle SuperSonics

Photography:
Fred Housel
Michael Shopenn

**University Child
Development School
Expansion
Seattle, Washington 2002**

Design Team:
Donald E. Carlson, FAIA
Steve Nordlund
Marc Roehrle
Trevor Schaaf
Sivichai Udomvoranun

Consultants:
Structural Engineer:
Skilling Ward Magnusson
Barkshire

Mechanical Engineer:
Sider & Byers Associates

Electrical Engineer:
Sparling Engineering

Civil Engineer:
Skilling Ward Magnusson
Barkshire

General Contractor:
RAFN Construction

Landscape Architect:
Pascoe Landscape Design

Surveyor:
Barghausen Consulting
Engineers, Inc.

Cost Estimator:
Robinson Company

Client:
University Child
Development School

**University of Washington
School of Social Work
Addition
Seattle, Washington 2000**

Design Team:
Donald E. Carlson, FAIA
Mark Withrow
Jim Hanford
Stewart Green
Jamal Salem

Consultants:
Structural Engineer:
Swenson Say Faget

Mechanical Engineer:
CDi Engineers

Electrical Engineer:
Sparling Engineering

Civil Engineer:
SvR Design Company

General Contractor:
Columbia Pacific

Landscape Architect:
SvR Design Company

Cost Estimator:
Robinson Company

Client:
University of Washington

Photography:
Fred Housel
Gregg Krogstad

**Wilcher Residence
Redmond,
Washington 2001**

Design Team:
Donald E. Carlson, FAIA
Dan Umbach
Marc Roehrle
Alyssa Shank
Taka Soga

Consultants:
Structural Engineer:
Joe Maw Engineering

General Contractor:
David Wailes Construction

Client:
Jim & Marty Wilcher

Photography:
Fred Housel

The making of architecture is a complex production that requires a cast of talented players, supporters, and critics. I would like to express my thanks and gratitude to our clients, friends, and to those individuals who have been pivotal to the realization of the work of our firm.

The old saying, "it takes a good client to make good architecture," is so true. We have been blessed with wonderful clients over the years. In many cases, projects would not have been realized without their support, dedication, and active participation. Each client appreciated the potential of good architecture, supported challenging ideas, and was eager to create something special. I would like to thank Larry and Suzi McKinney for the breakthrough opportunity in Larry's Markets; our independent school clients Roger Bass, Tom McCracken, Paula Smith, Melissa Masters, Paul Brenna, Al Snapp, Joan Booms, Jerry Milhon, and Frank Magusin. And I owe special thanks to two clients who persevered in their support of projects that challenged the aesthetic norm of their organizations-Thelma Kruse at Timberland Library and Bill Hager at the Port of Bellingham. The University of Washington has also been a proving ground and sponsor of our work. I especially want to thank Lee Copeland, Janet Donelson, Fred King, Doug Jennings, Athletic Director Barbara Hedges, and Social Work Dean Nancy Hooeyman and her facilities committee for their trust, support, and guidance.

I would like to acknowledge members of the firm, past and present, who have dedicated their time, talents, and enthusiasm to create the projects that established the firm's reputation for design excellence. Current key members include Mark Withrow, Jim Hanford, Eileen McHugh, Oschien Chen, Dan Umbach, Scott Hopkins, Steve Nordland, Erin Doherty, Nilla Conti, and Trevor Schaaf. Also thanks to former members for their contributions to the success of the firm-Lana Lisitsa, Allan Ferrin, Kevin Kane, Hal Eden, Terre Meinershagen, Gail Wong, Tom Morris, and Diane Jacobsen. The material for this monograph was painstakingly compiled by firm members Mark Withrow, Maya Leites, Greg Waddell, Bill Luria, Marc Roehrle, and Sivichai Udomvoranum—thank you.

I want especially to thank a few friends who appreciate our working style and architecture. Paul Schell, Buster Simpson, Jim Laser, Darrell Vange, Steve Elliott, and Bob Filley are our personal "cheerleaders" who provide support, advice, encouragement, and continually promote our work. In addition, getting projects published adds significantly to a firm's "currency." The architectural press has been a supporter of our work over the years. I would like to thank Deborah Dietsch, Reed Kroloff, Robert Ivy, Charles Linn, and Claire Enlow for their efforts in publishing our projects.

Finally, I'd like to express my appreciation and thanks to Frank Gehry and Greg Walsh. Frank taught me about "having a good eye"—with intuitive ideas, not only to look but to see—those gems that seem to come out of nowhere, and that "messy" is ok. Greg taught me how to "wield" a pencil and not worry that your forearm and hand were completely black by the end of the day.

Acknowledgements